Jeet Kune Do KICKBOXING

by Chris Kent and Tim Tackett

Published in the United States by
Know Now Publishing Company.

Manufactured in the United States of America

Library of Congress Catalog Card Number in process

ISBN: 0-938676-08-3

KNOW NOW PUBLISHING COMPANY
3932 So. Hill St., Los Angeles, CA 90037

DEDICATION

This book is dedicated to the Creator, who is responsible for all life and knowledge—and to Daniel Inosanto, whose friendship, guidance and caring showed us that the martial arts, like life itself, is a process, not a product.

ACKNOWLEDGEMENT

To everyone who has contributed to our growth as individuals and as martial artists, there are far too many to name. Our thanks to you all.

CONTENTS

Handwritten annotations:

S.A.A. (next to BASIC HAND TOOL / BASIC FOOT TOOL DEVELOPMENT)

A.B.C. (next to ATTACK BY COMBINATION)

P.I.A. (next to PROGRESSIVE INDIRECT ATTACK)

A.B.D. (next to ATTACK BY DRAWING)

H.I.A.

...ngle Angular Attack.
...tack By Combination
...rogressive Indirect Attack.
Attack By Drawing.
Hand Immobolisation Attack

3

BIOGRAPHY

Chris Kent

Chris Kent has been involved in martial arts for over 15 years. After studying Judo for two years and classical Gung Fu for one year, he was fortunate enough to become a student of Dan Inosanto in June 1973. At 17 he was the youngest member of Inosanto's backyard Jeet Kune Do class. In 1976 he received his Escrimador certificate, and in 1982 became a certified full instructor in both the Jun Fan Martial Arts and the Filipino Martial Arts. (With the exception of Dan Inosanto, no one has received certificates authorizing them in Jeet Kune Do as instructors.)

Apart from his duties as manager of the Inosanto Academy, Chris assists Dan in national and international martial arts seminars, as well as conducting his own seminars. His martial arts skills led to fight-oriented stunt work on television. In 1985, Chris formed his own company, "Combative Arts International," specializing in professional martial arts consultation and instruction. His students have included celebrities such as writer/producer/director Blake Edwards, and the creator of "Miami Vice," Anthony Yerkovich. He has also appeared in numerous martial arts books including "Jeet Kune Do—The Art and Philosophy of Bruce Lee" (where he is listed as a third-generation instructor), "The Balisong Manual," and "Jeet Kune Do—Entering to Trapping to Grappling" (Volumes 1 and 2), as well as numerous martial arts magazines.

Tim Tackett

This Jeet Kune Do and Filipino Martial Arts instructor has had a most varied martial arts background. Tim's martial arts training started in 1954 with Judo at the local YMCA. His serious training started in 1962 in Taiwan. While in Taiwan, Tackett studied Hsing-I Kung Fu, Chin Na, Tai Chi, and both Northern and Southern Shaolin boxing. After returning from Taiwan in 1965, he opened a Kung Fu school in Redlands, California. Tackett began in JKD when Dan Inosanto opened up his backyard to a few individuals following the closure of Bruce Lee's College Street school. He received the rank of Senior Jeet Kune Do student in 1973 from Dan Inosanto and graduated from the Filipino Kali Academy in 1976. Currently he is an associate instructor in Jun Fan Martial Arts and the Filipino Martial Arts. Like many JKD students, Tackett has also received supplemental training in Wing Chun, Western wrestling and boxing, and Thai boxing.

Tackett is married and the father of two grown children. He earned a Master of Fine Arts degree in drama from the University of California at Riverside, where he graduated a member of Phi Beta Kappa. He is now a drama teacher at Montclair High School in Montclair, California.

Tackett restricts his teaching to a small, nonprofit "backyard" class in Redlands, California, and seminars around the country. He has also been an innovator in applying JKD principles to football and has worked with both the Dallas Cowboys and the San Francisco 49ers. Tackett is the author of two books on Hsing-I Kung Fu and is co-author with Larry Hartsell of "Jeet Kune Do—Entering to Trapping to Grappling."

Tim Tackett, Jr.

Tim has been studying the martial arts for 12 years, since the age of 10. His first instructor was his father, Tim Tackett, Sr. Tim began his training at the Filipino Kali Academy under Tony Luna in 1975. Tim received apprentice instructor certificates in the Jun Fan arts and Eskrima from Dan Inosanto in 1983. Tim has assisted his father in seminars around the country, and has worked with both the Dallas Cowboys and the San Francisco 49ers. Tim attends the University of California at Riverside, where he is majoring in Environmental Science.

Jeff Imada

Jeff Imada is a certified full instructor in both the Jun Fan and Filipino Martial Arts under Dan Inosanto. He is also a professional stunt actor/coordinator with numerous television and feature film credits. He is the author of "The Balisong Manual," and serves as a technical advisor to Pacific Cutlery Corporation.

INTRODUCTION

Regardless of their origins, the practice of martial arts is still basically an athletic endeavor, in that it requires body movement. And as such, they follow similar biomechanical principles in developing such qualities as skill, speed, coordination, etc. It is both physical and mental, and to neglect one in favor of the other is to fall short of one's fullest potential.

A martial artist is therefore an athlete, and just as there are different levels of athletes such as amateurs, semi-professional and professional, there are various types of martial artists. There are those who pursue martial arts professionally, with the hopes of a career as a fighter or a teacher, or both. There are those who practice it for recreation, or as a hobby. And there are some who merely wish to learn how to defend themselves should it ever be necessary. Whatever one's reasons for studying a fighting art, the purpose of this book is to aid in the martial artist's personal development.

While one cannot learn Jeet Kune Do from a book, you can gain helpful insight into some of the training methods used to develop different qualities required to become proficient in kickboxing. And even if it may be true that there is no such thing as a definite method of fighting, there is still a definite training progression, a direction to get from Point A to Point B.

The acquisition of skill is a primary consideration in the basic development of all martial artists. What we give are learning experiences rather than technique upon technique. The emphasis is placed upon the continual building up of precision, rhythm, synchronization while augmenting speed progressively. This progression can be listed as:

1. Synchronization with self.
2. Synchronization with training partner or opponent.
3. Synchronization with all types of opponents.

The ability to "fit in" with any opponent is the long-term training goal.

Sparring is like a game of physical chess. It can be compared to a conversation between two individuals in which an exchange of dialogue continues back and forth, until it is ended somehow. It is both rhythmic and unrhythmic, and it includes pauses, interruptions, etc. When you are sparring you have to problem-solve. It requires instant analysis, decision making, speed in carrying out an action in a fraction of a second, and the ability to react and adjust to the situation as it changes. Only by having a comprehensive understanding of the basic tools available can you then concentrate on the more technical aspects such as timing, distance, and so on.

By limiting the tools to be used in a training session, or manipulating the environment in which the training takes place, we create learning experiences which can develop different skills at different times. One is only limited by their own imagination in creating different learning situations.

This book is laid out in the following manner:

(a) Two chapters that illustrate the basic punching and kicking tools. And various methods to aid in their development. These can be classified as single attacks.

(b) One chapter devoted to each of the ways of attack by combination, progressive indirect attack, attack by drawing (except trapping which is well covered in Larry Hartsell's books).

(c) One chapter demonstrating various training methods and drills that a martial artist can use to achieve a well-rounded basic proficiency in kickboxing.

But understand that this is not a book of techniques. The photographs and text are used to illustrate examples of some of the concepts used in JKD. There are many, many others. And each combative motion must be studied, analyzed and made your own.

There is a saying that "Insecure people seek to indoctrinate, whereas secure people seek to educate." This book is not meant to be taken as gospel truth. Rather, it is meant to be used as a training aid, a coaching guide, and to shed some light on some of the various training methods we use. What you get out of this book will be entirely up to you, the individual martial artist. There are many schools of thought in martial arts, each possessing strengths and weaknesses. You should look around to as many other sources as you can for knowledge and remember that this is only one aspect of the total JKD picture, and that no one "has it all."

MY FOLLOWERS IN JEET KUNE DO, DO LISTEN TO THIS... ALL FIXED SET PATTERN ARE INCAPABLE OF ADAPTABILITY OR PLIABILITY. THE TRUTH IS OUTSIDE OF ALL FIXED PATTERNS.

Bruce Lee 1966

HISTORY

Bruce Lee's kickboxing phase began in 1965 when he moved to Los Angeles from Oakland to pursue his acting career. Prior to that time he was Jun Fan/Wing Chun oriented.

Dan Inosanto was among a small handful of students that Bruce taught privately in his living room between 1965 and 1966. In late '66, Bruce began to conduct small semi-public Gung-Fu classes behind Wayne Chan's Pharmacy in Los Angeles Chinatown. In 1967 the Chinatown school on College Street was opened. It was during this time that Bruce Lee's kickboxing era flourished.

The secret "closed-door sessions" were devoted to physical conditioning and tool development, utilizing all types of training equipment like focus gloves, heavy bags, top and bottom bags and football shields. *Everything* was contact oriented and sparring was the crucible, the ultimate testing ground that all the students had worked on in training. Basic trapping, sensitivity and various types of sparring were used (one on one, two vs. one, etc.) to develop timing and distance.

The arts influencing the kickboxing phase were diverse in structure and origin. Western boxing, Thai boxing, Savate, Northern and Southern Gung-Fu kicking, Sikaran, modified Wing Chun, among others, were used.

The use of body armor was used for safety during full contact sparring in the early days, but was gradually eliminated as the kickboxing progressed. No strict uniform dress code ever existed,

with students wearing anything they wanted, even construction boots.

In 1970, Dan Inosanto greatly influenced the curriculum by adding Filipino boxing (Panantukan). There were two reasons for the addition. First, it added more sophistication to the Western boxing and secondly, it added the ability to drill realistically and combatively without each student bashing the other's face in every workout. The Filipino training methods were developed from their stick-fighting methods to allow a student to "survive" in training.

Since then, many new training drills and methods were synthesized into the kickboxing curriculum. Like modern athletics, older methods are updated and changed where necessary, while fundamental principles remain. Students learn body mechanics and body motion and then "make it their own." What each individual chooses may be different—some favor hands over feet, some favor feet over hands, but they all learn to understand the strengths and weaknesses of each facet.

As in athletics, to comprehend what a martial artist does, to appreciate how he pursues his art, you must understand the art. You must speak the language. And the martial artist should be able to communicate effectively in his chosen medium of expression. That is why Jeet Kune Do has remained so long a mystery to so many people. It is one art, but expresses itself in many languages. It is a strangely complex and mystifying animal. What is attempted here is to de-mystify it a little.

Like any formidable opponent, the animal must become known before it can be challenged with any surety of success. To know it, you must study and observe it. Not for weeks or months, but every day for years. Even with knowledge and training more is required. Maturity and a deep comprehension of combative principles are necessary. The animal is cunning, continually changing, forever adapting.

What is so time-consuming is not so much the mastering of each of the individual elements involved, but understanding and embracing the total concept. To the unknowledgeable observer JKD may only appear to be various separate elements such as boxing, wrestling, Wing Chun, loosely strung together to create one generalized martial art. But that is an illusion, and to embrace the illusion is to invite defeat. It is a single entity, both an art and a science, and understanding that in all its ramifications is the key to successfully engaging and doing battle with the animal. It must be understood. It must dictate the plan for training, and permeate every hour of the martial artist's study.

The animal is a whole with many parts, commitment to any single portion of which will detract from the rest.

So how does one go about studying the animal? The same way one would approach any athletic endeavor. Combative situations combine different elements, and change from moment to moment. It may stress speed one moment, strength the next, then resilience, then endurance.

Every one of the combative skills has its own technique, its own motion that must be developed and perfected, the right move at the right time. In any physical movement there is always a most efficient and lively manner to carry it out, that is regarding leverage, balance, economical use of motion. It must be learned first, the same way one learns a lesson. But then it must be taken beyond that level. A martial artist thinks while learning, and that is how it should be. In an actual fight situation there will be little or no time for thoughts. By then each action must be second nature to the individual, the same way he brushes an annoying fly away from his face. This automaticity of response is what one seeks.

In a time of narrowing expertise and specialization, the JKD practitioner is the super all-rounder—a martial artist whose specialty is the overall picture. Such an accomplishment requires a tremendous commitment of energy and training.

The incredible diversity of combat means that JKD training is intentionally general in scope. Particular emphasis may be placed on different aspects at different times in order to increase a student's awareness in these various arenas. But the essence is to understand a particular art in order to be able to deal with it—not to become a 'boxer' or a 'wrestler'. It is to enter into their realm, experience it, but not be caught up in it. Unfortunately this is where a lot of people fall into a trap and start to think that "boxing is where it's at." It is 'a' truth, not 'the' truth. All arts have advantages and disadvantages, none possesses everything.

A JKD practitioner cannot study 10 times as hard or 10 times as long as a martial artist who specializes in one method. He must train 10 times as smart. The ultimate goal is to get as good as your genetic potential will allow in each of the elements—and to be able to shift from one to another without stopping the mind to think about it. And sparring is the testing ground for the street.

The animal is yourself. The essence is to be in command of your body, to make it do what you want it to do when you want it to do it. That's what JKD is about, and what makes it "uniquely complicated simplicity."

BASIC HAND TOOL DEVELOPMENT

To use an analogy related to warfare, in JKD we often refer to the legs as the heavy artillery and the arms as the infantry. In military tactics, when an army wishes to conquer a city, there are certain methods. You may stay outside the city all day long and shell it with heavy artillery. But, regardless of the damage you may inflict, in order to take the city, you must still go in with the infantry.

For this reason the development of one's punching tools is of paramount importance. There are many types of punches, all of which should be learned to be thrown from a variety of angles, and combined with footwork and body motion to make them more effective.

For instance, there are several types of lead jabs. Which one a fighter chooses to use is dependent upon the situation. The wider his punching arsenal is, the more choices he will have.

Some punches may be classified as minor blows in that, while they are not ordinarily designed to knock out an opponent, they aid in setting up a major or knockout blow.

Learn and practice punching with economy of motion, accuracy, and from a variety of angles, both singly and in combination.

BASIC HAND TOOLS WITH EQUIPMENT

THE BASIC JKD STANCE (Bai Joing)

This stance is the basic JKD stance. Both feet are at approximately a 45-degree angle. The front foot is turned inwards to help protect the groin. The rear foot is at an angle to help (as we'll see later) the power of the punch. The rear heel is raised to help give a springing action to your footwork and to help make you a more elusive target. The toe of the front foot and the heel of your rear foot should be on the same line.

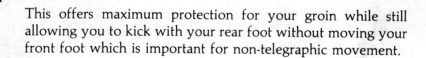

This offers maximum protection for your groin while still allowing you to kick with your rear foot without moving your front foot which is important for non-telegraphic movement.

Both knees should bend to add strength to your stance and flexibility and speed to your movements. The width of stance will vary according to individual preference keeping within the principles that the stance should not be too short to be weak or too long to be static or rigid. At the beginning level you should keep your weight approximately 50 percent on each leg.

The hand positions are not static but will vary from both hands held high to the front hand held low to protect the low line while the rear hand is high to protect the high line.

The important thing about the basic JKD stance is that it is never static. It is meant to be a stance you can deliver a powerful attack from while at the same time a stance that you can move from to avoid your opponent's attack.

Step to your right with your front foot.

From the basic stance you can:

Step to your left with your rear foot.

Step forward with your front foot while angling to the right.

Step forward with your rear foot while angling to the left.

14

All of the above pictures show the JKD stance with the right foot forward. Most right-handed JKD practitioners prefer the right lead for the following reasons.

1. **Since the front hand is used for the stop hit (see below) it makes sense to have your most powerful hand forward.**
2. **Since the front leg is used for the stop kick (see below) the same reason applies.**
3. **Since your left hand is weaker it makes sense to carry farther back so it will have further to travel to the target and will gather more momentum which will give it more power.**

The left-handed fighter will of course prefer the left lead. Many right-handed JKD fighters because of Western boxing training or personal preference will be more comfortable fighting mainly out of a left lead while many will shift from left to right lead.

Since an important JKD principle is whatever works for the individual, you should practice using both leads. While most of the techniques used in the book are done from the right lead, you should give equal time to working these techniques out of a left lead also. Then you can see what will work best for you in any given situation.

FRONT HAND TOOLS

FLICKER JAB

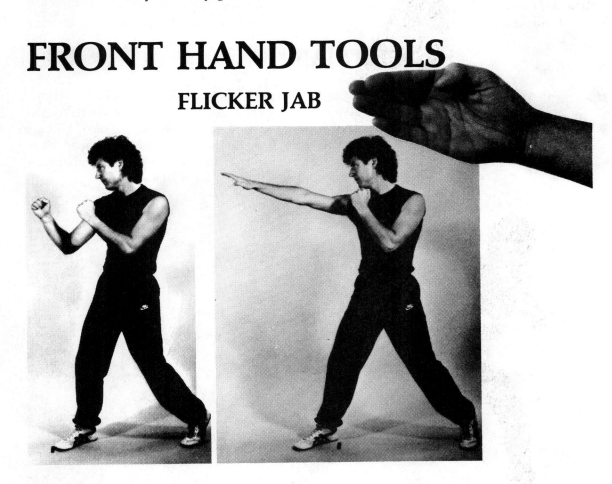

The flicker jab is the fastest jab. It is also the weakest jab. Since it is a weak jab it is usually used as a finger jab to the eyes. Since it is so fast and requires little energy, it is also used as a probe to test your opponent's defense or as a fake to set up an attack to another line.

To perform the flicker jab shoot your hand out from the elbow directly to your opponent's eyes while keeping as relaxed as possible. To gain a little more power transfer some of your weight to your front leg. As soon as you finish your flicker jab you should immediately follow with another attack or return to the on guard position.

Depending on distance, the flicker jab can be done from a stationary stance or you can take a slight step forward with your front foot.

THE SPEED JAB

The speed jab is a more powerful jab than the flicker jab. To perform the speed jab shoot your hand to the target by throwing your shoulder forward. You can do the speed jab from a stationary stance or by taking a short step forward with your front foot as pictured. The speed jab is usually used to keep your opponent off balance, to set up another technique, or to keep your opponent from moving toward you.

Any jab can be done from a low guard to a high guard position.

 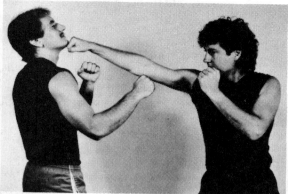

Speed jab from a high guard.

Speed jab from a low guard.

THE POWER JAB

The power jab is one of the most powerful of the front hand tools. The power jab starts with a powerful twist of your rear foot which transfers most of your weight to your front leg. Make sure your hip as well as your shoulder thrust forward. This can also be done from a stationary stance or you can step forward with your front foot as pictured. When you step forward make sure your rear foot pushes forward. If hitting with a horizontal fist, as pictured, twist your fist on impact, since it requires more energy to throw a power jab, and it takes more of a commitment. It takes longer to recover from throwing this type of jab. With this in mind, make sure you have a clear opening before throwing a power jab.

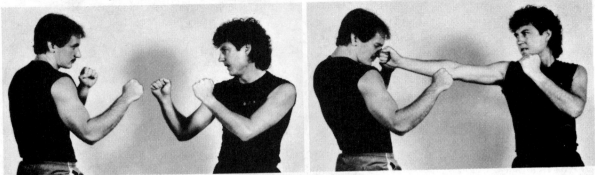

The power jab can also be done with a vertical fist to the nose like a Wing Chun punch.

THE ENTERING LEAD

The entering lead is used to bridge the gap, to move from kicking range to hand range. It is also used to enter to trapping or grappling range. You can do the entering lead with a flicker, speed, or power jab.

To do the entering lead push off hard with your rear foot as you step forward with your front foot. Your fist should make contact a split second before your foot hits the ground. The rear foot then slides forward. All of this is done in a split second.

18

THE DEFENSIVE JAB

As its name suggests the defensive jab is used to defend against an attack. As your opponent attempts to hit you with a hard attack, drop your weight back on to your rear leg as you jab with your front hand.

WHIPPING JAB

The whipping jab is performed much like the power jab. The main difference is that after you make contact with a power jab, your hand returns straight back to the on guard position, but as you make contact with the whipping jab your arm snaps to the inside.

While this snapping action will add a powerful momentum to your punch it will also leave you open to your opponent's rear hand. Make sure there is a target and that you can hit it before you attempt this punch.

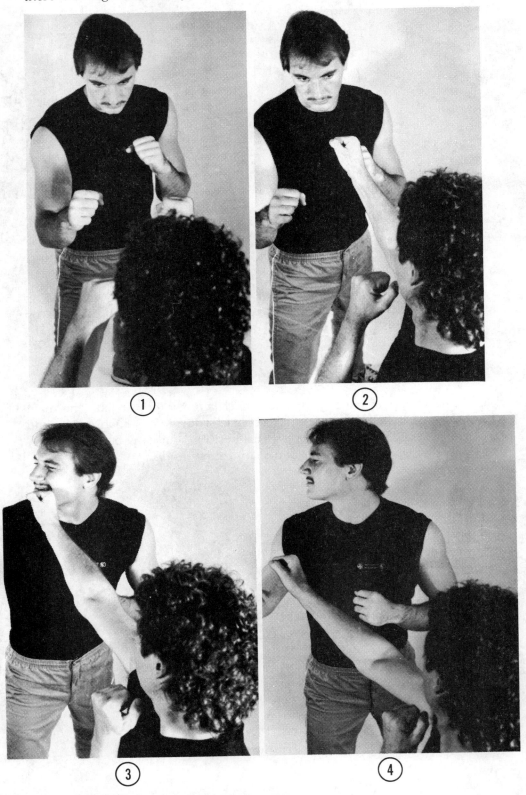

1
2
3
4

GENERAL JAB PRINCIPLES

1. Keep relaxed as you throw the jab. Try and keep the bicep relaxed.
2. Do not focus your punch, instead hit through your target.
3. Do not cock your fist back before you punch as this will telegraph the punch. Rather punch from where your hand is.
4. Make sure you cover your head with the rear hand.

Depending on your relationship to your opponent, your cover can be on the left side of your head.

Or the right side of your head.

5. Remember you can angle your body as you punch. You can do this as you slip a punch or to make yourself a more elusive target.

Straight

Angle to the right

Angle to the left

6. You can hit to the inside or the outside of your opponent's cover depending on how he covers.

Hitting on the inside line

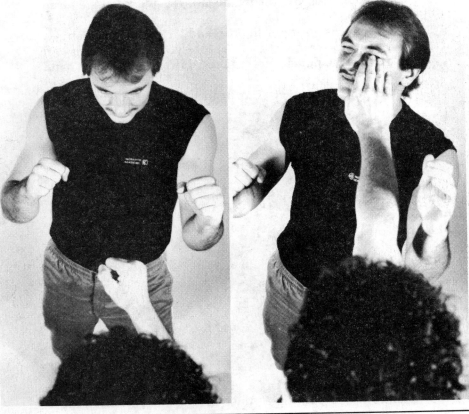

Hitting on the outside line

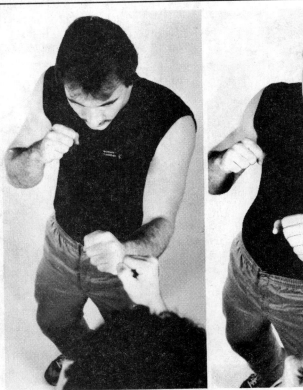

7. The angle of the fist on impact can vary. Experiment on this.

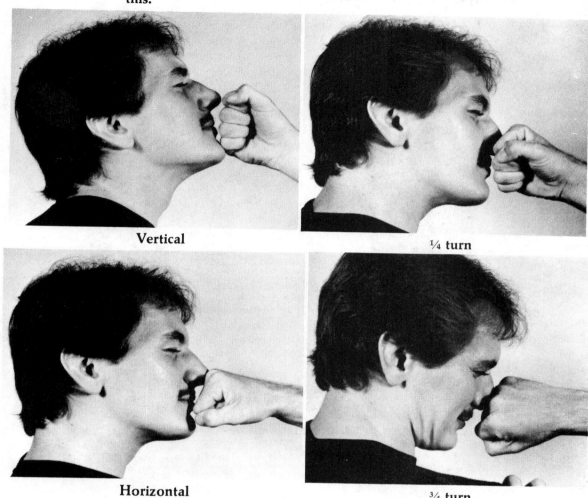

Vertical

¼ turn

Horizontal

¾ turn

8. Besides your fist you can hit with other areas of your hand.

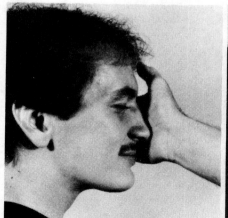

Jab with side palm

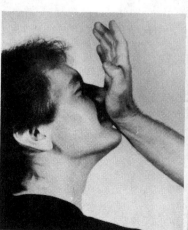

Jab with straight palm

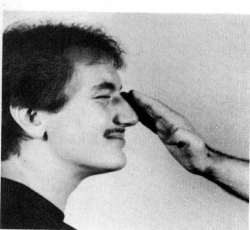

Finger jab

MAJOR JAB ERRORS

Avoid the following errors when you jab:

First let's review the correct form for the jab

Correct jab side view

Correct jab front view

JAB ERRORS

1. Lifting the rear foot off of the ground will weaken your punch and make it more difficult to recover.

2. Lowering your rear guard will not add to your power and will leave you open to a counterattack.

3. Dropping your front shoulder will also leave you open. If you drop your front shoulder and your rear guard, your whole head will be exposed.

4. If you cross your centerline you will be open to a rear hand counter.

5. **If you drop your front hand after you jab, you will also create an opening.**
6. **If you raise your elbow you will weaken the punch and expose your ribs to a counterattack.**

JAB TO THE BODY

While the body jab is usually used as a probe or a fake, it can be effective as the first punch in a combination attack.

The body jab side view

To do a body jab from a right lead. While stepping forward with your right foot drive your fist into your opponent's ribs. Make sure you angle to your left and cover the right side of your head with your rear hand. By angling and covering you make it more difficult for your opponent to counterattack.

Rear view

THE LEAD HOOK

The lead hook to the head can be thrown at three ranges.

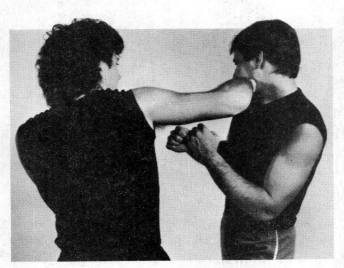

Tight hook

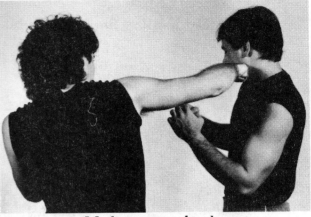

Medium range hook

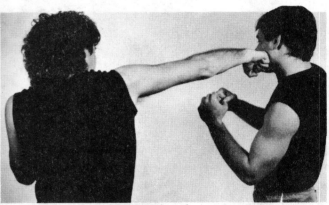

Loose hook

Which hook you use depends on your distance to your target. Whichever hook you throw, the principles of how you throw it will remain the same. To throw the hook drop your rear heel to the ground as you lift your front heel off the ground. At the same time pivot your hip to the right as you raise your right elbow and punch. As you throw a hook punch imagine you are turning in a barrel. When you hook make sure your arm is parallel to the ground and that your rear hand covers the left side of your head.

Your power will come from the weight transfer to your rear leg and the pivot of your hip.

The angle of your fist on impact can be:

Vertical   Or horizontal

COMMON HOOK ERRORS

ERRORS:

The correct hook (tight front view)

Turning the front foot over will weaken the **punch** because you are no longer punching "**from the ground.**"

Too much follow through will leave you too **open for a** counterattack.

Too wide a swing will also leave you open.

Having your shoulder too far forward will also weaken the punch.

The correct angle of the shoulder

If the elbow is down the hook will be weaker and easier to block.

Correct angle of elbow.

THE SHOVEL HOOK

The shovel hook is a close range punch. As you punch you drop your weight on your foot as you lift your front heel off of the ground. The front hand shoots at an angle to the ribs or solar plexus. The action is similar to unloading a heavy shovel full of dirt. The shovel hook is almost always a body punch.

THE UPPERCUT

The target for the uppercut can either be the body or the chin. Like a shovel hook, the uppercut is also a close range weapon used for infighting. It is thrown just like the shovel hook, except it comes straight up while the shovel hook angles in.

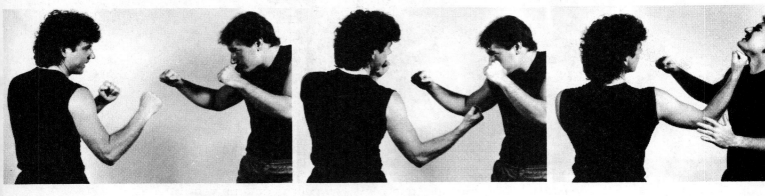

THE BACK FIST

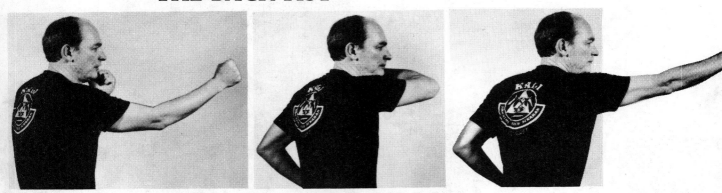

The classical back fist

The problem with the classical back fist is that when you cock the hand back you leave yourself open to your opponent's rear hand.

The JKD back fist

The JKD backfist is more efficient. Instead of cocking your hand back, bring your hip forward as you put your weight onto your front leg. This will give you the speed, the power, and the angle to make this an efficient tool for combat.

The back fist can be done with the knuckles.

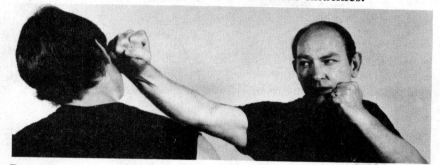

But since you can injure the back of your hand if you come in contact with your opponent's skull, it is recommended that you use a hammer fist.

THE STRAIGHT REAR (CROSS)

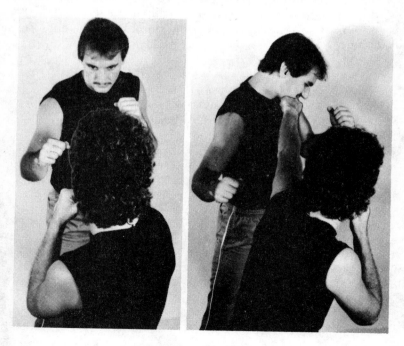

The straight arrow

The straight rear, also called the straight arrow, is a powerful punch. To throw this punch pivot your rear foot as you shoot your hand directly to your opponent's chin or nose. The whole left side of your body should act like a slamming door. The power comes from the pivot of the rear foot which pivots the rear hip which transfers the weight to the front leg. Unlike the classical reverse punch, the straight rear extends the shoulder. This shoulder extension adds power and distance to your punch.

THE CROSS

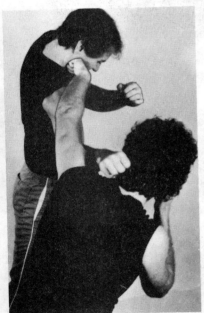

The cross is thrown when your opponent attempts to jab you. It requires a lot of practice and perfect timing to work. It is thrown just like a straight rear except it curves slightly as it "crosses" over your opponent's lead jab. You should slip inside your opponent's jab as your opponent crosses.

THE OVERHEAD

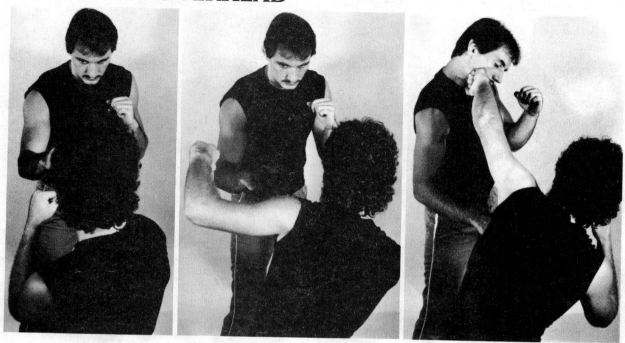

The overhead is thrown just like the straight arrow except the elbow raises and the punch loops to the target. The power comes from the momentum of your body as it drives forward.

THE LOW CROSS

To the inside line

To the outside line

THE REAR HOOK TO THE HEAD

This is thrown just like the lead hook, except that it is almost always a tight hook and you twist your rear foot to get power.

REAR SHOVEL HOOK

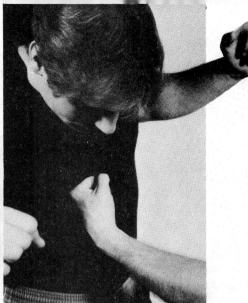

This is the same as the lead shovel hook except that the rear heel lifts up as the weight transfers to the front leg.

REAR UPPERCUT

The body mechanics of the rear uppercut are the same as the rear shovel hook.

REAR BACK FIST

To get the proper angle to throw the rear back fist twist your body to the right and transfer your weight to your front foot as you throw your rear hip into the punch.

BASIC USE OF FOCUS GLOVES

The focus glove is one of the most valuable pieces of training equipment available today. If used correctly, you can come very close to actually sparring, and use every possible punch. "Feeding" the focus gloves is an art in itself. A good feeder can use the gloves to make his partner work both offensive and defensive punching actions, develop his sense of timing, learn correct distancing for his punches, and increase mobility.

In the following examples we start from a stationary position with the gloves set, in order for the partner to learn visual recognition (what punches can be thrown at each glove when it is in a particular position). Then we progress to showing the glove to the partner from a neutral position (similar to using "flash cards" in school).

Training with the focus gloves can be done with: (a) the feeder remaining stationary, and (b) the feeder moving around. You are only limited by your own imagination in how to use the gloves.

STATIONARY FOCUS GLOVE

Holding the focus glove to practice distance and power of the various hand tools.

1. Jab or Cross

Front view   **Side view**

**2. Jab, Cross, Hook
   or Jab, Hook, Cross
   or Jab, Hook
   or Cross, Hook**

Front view   Side view

**3. Jab, Cross, Low Hook
   or Jab, Low Hook, Cross**

4. Jab, Cross, Uppercut

5. High Jab, Low Cross or High to Low Jab

Front view   Side view

6. Front and Rear Uppercuts

7. Low to High Hook

HITTING THE FOCUS GLOVE WITH A
SINGLE DIRECT ATTACK (SDA)

1. The Jab

2. The Cross

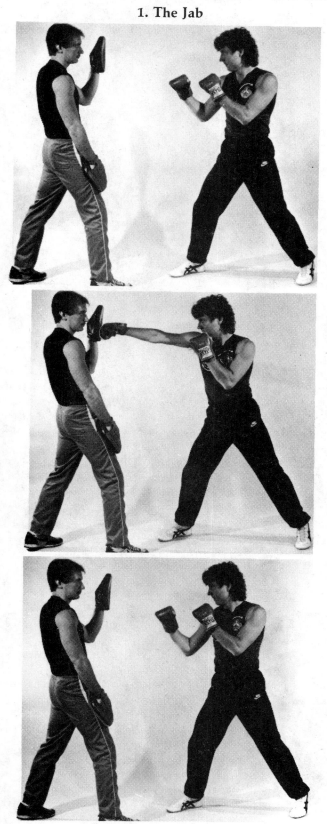

3. The Hook

4. The Uppercut

THE FOCUS GLOVE FOR REACTION TRAINING

The focus glove can be used for stimulus-response training. This type of training is for speed, reaction, and speed of choice of the proper tool. To do this type of training hold the focus gloves in a neutral position with the rear glove on your chest and the front glove on your front thigh. Then move the glove or gloves to one of the examples shown.

HOW TO FEED FOR SINGLE DIRECT ATTACK (SDA)

1. Jab or Cross

2. High Hook

3. Low Hook

4. Uppercut

Below are some examples of reaction training in action.

1.   Cross

2.   Cross to High Hook

From here on the neutral position will not be shown.

3.   Jab to Low Hook

44

4. Cross to Uppercut

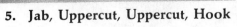
5. Jab, Uppercut, Uppercut, Hook

BASIC FOOT TOOL DEVELOPMENT

The use of the leg as a striking tool offers two major advantages. The first is longer reach, which enables you to score an attack from a greater distance. The second is more power, for it is a basic physiological fact that the legs are naturally much stronger than the arms. This is why we sometimes refer to the legs as heavy artillery.

Unfortunately, when it comes to kickboxing, most fighters resort to always slugging with their feet, as opposed to boxing with them.

As with punching, different kicks can be used to accomplish different goals. Some kicks may be used as minor attacks in order to set up a major attack, be it another kick or even a punch.

A good kicking repertoire makes it more difficult for an opponent to reach you with his hands, giving you a larger "aura of safety."

As with punching, kicking should be learned from a variety of angles, with both feet, and combined with footwork and body angulation.

THE STRAIGHT KICK

Below you can see the number of frames needed to do a straight kick in a classical manner. Bruce Lee felt that chambering the kick did nothing for power and made the kick inefficient by telegraphing it.

THE JKD STRAIGHT GROIN KICK

Slide up with your rear leg. At the same time snap your front leg up into your opponent's groin. Don't chamber the kicking leg. The bend of the knee will feel natural, don't worry about it. The power comes from a rising action of your hip as well as the short snap of your knee. Make sure you cover your head with your rear hand.

Kick with instep or shin

Kick with the toe

After your kick you can either bring your front foot back which will return you to your original position, or you can step directly down with your front foot as you use a hand attack.

THE FRONT THRUST KICK

This is the same as the snap kick except that the hip thrusts forward.

HOOK KICK

While most martial arts call this a roundhouse kick, we call it a hook kick because it follows the same line as a hook punch.

The classical roundhouse kick

There are less moves to the JKD hook kick. The power of the hook kick comes from the twisting action of your rear foot, the twist of your front hip, and the short snap of your knee. On any JKD kick hit through the target. Stay relaxed. DO NOT FOCUS. Keep your rear hand up to protect your head. Make contact with your toe, instep, or shin.

THE JKD HOOK KICK

To the groin with an upward angle

To the ribs with an inward or upward angle

To the neck with a downward angle

SIDE KICK

The basic side kick is done with the natural bend of the front knee as you slide your rear leg forward. The power comes from the hip as well as the body momentum moving forward. Again, don't focus. Hit through the target. Make contact with the flat of the heel or the whole flat of the foot.

If you work this kick it will become too powerful to use the classical blade of the foot to make contact as you can break your ankle.

THE JKD SIDE KICK

Down angle to shin or knee

Straight angle to body

Upward angle to face

The angle-in side kick

This is good to do when you are in an unmatched stance to your opponent. Step out with your right foot so that you can angle in to the exposed portion of your opponent's body, in this case his stomach.

THE INVERTED HOOK KICK

This kick is used as a front leg attack to the groin when you're in an unmatched stance. Slide up with your rear foot. Bring your front leg into your opponent's groin at an oblique angle. The power comes from the hip turning outward.

HEEL HOOK KICK

This kick can be done two ways, with whipping action of the knee or with a straight leg.

Straight leg heel hook kick

Whipping heel hook kick

Rear view

56

THE REAR LEG HOOK KICK

This is a power kick and is thrown similar to how the Thai boxers throw their round kick. The kick is usually thrown to the thigh, ribs or neck and the contact point is with your shin. The power comes from the twist of your front foot and the torque of your hip. As in any fully committed technique it is hard to fake or change the line with this kick. A good Thai boxer can generate a force of over 200 pounds with this kick.

The fully committed rear leg hook kick

The one half committed rear leg hook kick

This looks like the above kick except that the front foot does not torque as much, and the power is less. This kick is used as a probe, to bridge the gap, to fake or harass.

Quick rear hook kick with cover

This is a fast kick which returns to its original position. Make sure to retract the leg quickly.

REAR SIDE KICK

Since this is a relatively slow kick, it is seldom done above the knee.

STRAIGHT REAR

With step down into hand range

The power comes from your hip as well as the snapping action of your knee. Make sure you hit with your hand a split second before your foot hits the ground.

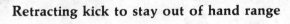
Retracting kick to stay out of hand range

If your opponent blocks your kick you can be in his hand range.

If you don't want to be in hand range, bring your kicking foot in front of your other foot.

OBLIQUE

The straight oblique comes from the floor to your opponent's knee with a lifting action.

With the stomping oblique you raise your rear knee and stomp down on your opponent's foot.

SPIN KICK

The spinning side kick

Spin on your front foot and do a side kick.

Side rear

If you extend your hip you do a side rear kick.

Spinning heel hook kick

This is a heel hook kick done from a spin.

FOOTWORK FOR FRONT LEAD KICK

The footwork you use for a kick depends on range, follow-ups or terrain.

Slide

Slide your rear foot forward as you kick.

Step and slide

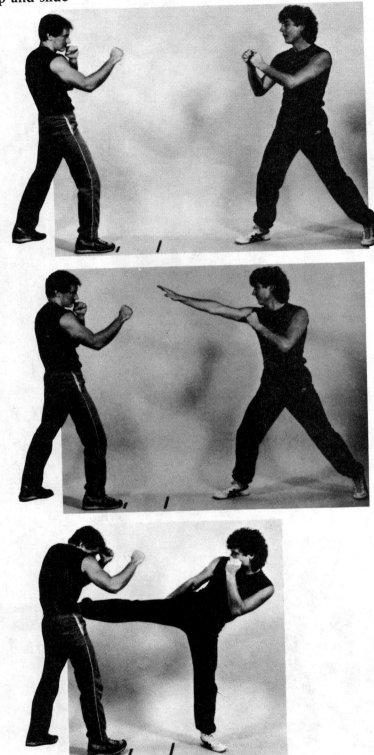

If you are too far away for a slide kick, take a short step forward with your front foot making sure you disguise the step with a front finger jab. Then slide and kick.

Pendulum

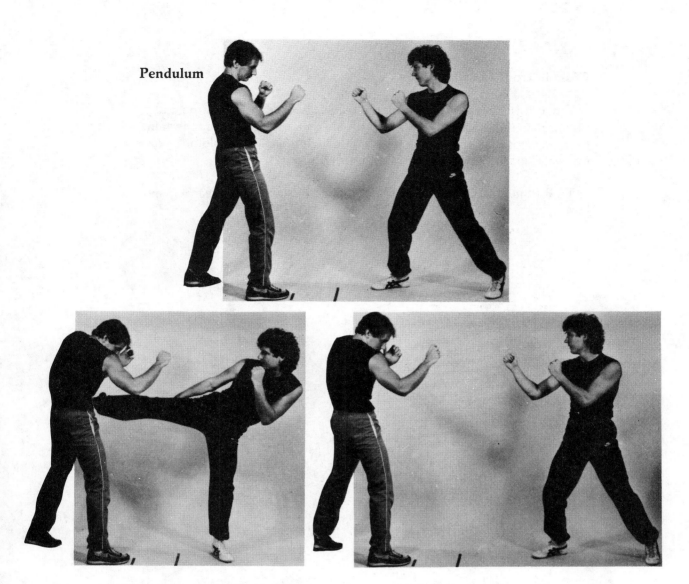

This is used to bridge the gap and return to your original position, thus staying out of hand range. After you slide and kick, bring your front foot back to your original position. In effect your front foot acts like the pendulum of a clock.

Lead switch

Slide up with the rear leg as you kick with the front. After you kick you can switch leads by bringing your front foot all the way back.

Cross in front and kick

While this footwork and the cross behind (see below) are structurally slower than the slide footwork, they should be learned because of terrain. Examples of terrain where the slide would be impractical would be an icy sidewalk, gravel, or any slippery or uneven surface.

To do the cross in front, simply cross in front with your rear leg and kick.

Cross behind

This is the same as the cross in front except that the rear leg crosses behind the front.

Usually a hook kick will "feel" better with a cross in front, and a side kick will "feel" better with a cross behind. This is because of the angle of your hip.

FOOTWORK FOR REAR LEG KICK

Step through

The step through bridges the gap and places you in hand range. Here we see a step through hook kick followed by a jab.

Retracting

The retracting allows you to kick with your rear leg and by bringing it back to your original position, you can stay out of hand range.

Lead switch with pendulum

By adding a pendulum with your kicking leg, you can stay out of hand range and switch leads.

70

BASIC USE OF TRAINING EQUIPMENT

The use of various types of training equipment for kicking is to aid in developing an immediate relationship to an opponent, a feel of hitting something. Each piece of equipment has advantages and disadvantages. But if used correctly, the equipment is invaluable for training one's kicking skills. The following sequences illustrate the training of basic kicks utilizing focus gloves and the kicking shield. Other equipment such as heavy bags, and Thai pads can and should be used also. In the beginning stages the equipment holder should remain in a stationary position, but once the martial artist is competent in using basic kicks, the holder should begin to move around as he sets different targets. This way the kicker learns to relate to a moving target.

Work on economical motions in delivering your kicks, quick recovery and well-covered positioning.

FOCUS GLOVE

SINGLE DIRECT ATTACK (SDA)

Front kick

Hook kick

Side kick

Inverted hook kick

Heel hook

KICKING SHIELD
SINGLE DIRECT ATTACK (SDA)
Front kick

Side kick

Hook kick

Inverted hook

Rear hook kick

Spin kick

ATTACK BY COMBINATION (ABC)

An attack by combination may be defined as a series of two or more attacking motions that flow from one to another naturally, and are usually thrown to more than one target area.

Utilizing the hands and feet either separately or in combination, they are compound attacks, employed in a well-planned series, with each opening creating another.

Although used in conjunction with feints and all other forms of attack such as single direct attack, in attack by combination each blow in the series is intended to score. This requires economical motion, tight defense, speed and surprise, and determination in execution.

Most combinations have a rhythmic feel to the series. However, the rhythm of any series can be varied by either speeding up or slowing down the tempo of one or more of the blows being thrown.

HAND-HAND (H-H)

Below are just a few of the many H-H combinations.

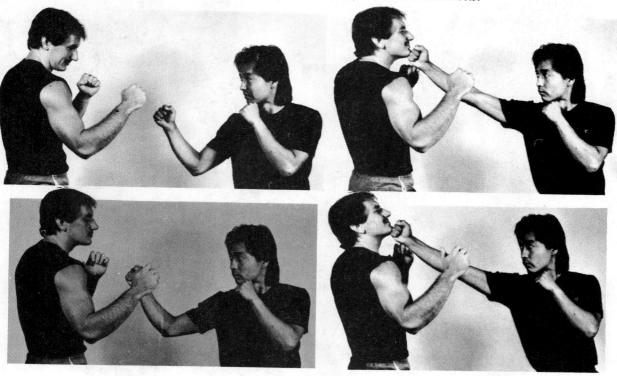

Double Jab

Low to High Jab

Jab to Cross

Jab to Low Cross

Jab to High Hook

HAND-FOOT (H-F)

Below are a few examples of (H-F) combinations.

Jab to Low Side Kick

Jab to Hook Kick

Jab to Inverted Hook Kick

Jab to Spin Kick

Jab to Rear Hook Kick

FOOT-HAND (F-H)

Below are just a few examples of possible (F-H) combinations.

Hook Kick to Jab

Hook Kick to Back Fist

Hook Kick to Hook Punch

ATTACK BY COMBINATION (ABC)
FOOT-FOOT (F-F) USING FOCUS GLOVES

Below are just a few examples of how to use focus gloves for ABC kicking.

Front Kick to Hook Kick

After your front kick makes contact with the focus glove, your partner quickly places the glove in a vertical position, you then do a hook kick without your kicking foot touching the ground.

Another way to do this combination is to have your partner slide back after the front kick. You then have to plant your front foot and slide up and hook kick (not shown).

The first one would be a combination if your opponent stands and blocks. The second one is used if he retreats from your front kick.

Hook Kick to Side Kick

Front Hook Kick to Rear Hook Kick

F-F ON THE SHIELD

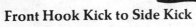

Front Hook Kick to Side Kick

Side Kick to Spin Kick

Front Hook Kick to Rear Hook Kick

HITTING THE FOCUS GLOVE WITH AN ATTACK BY COMBINATION (ABC)

Below are just three examples of the many ABC hand attacks that are possible.

Jab, Cross, Hook

Jab, Hook, Cross

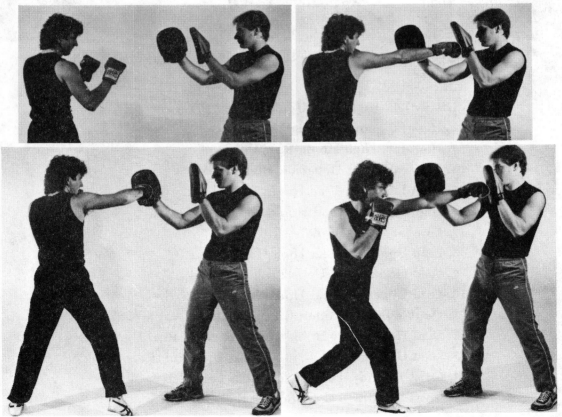

Jab, Cross, Uppercut

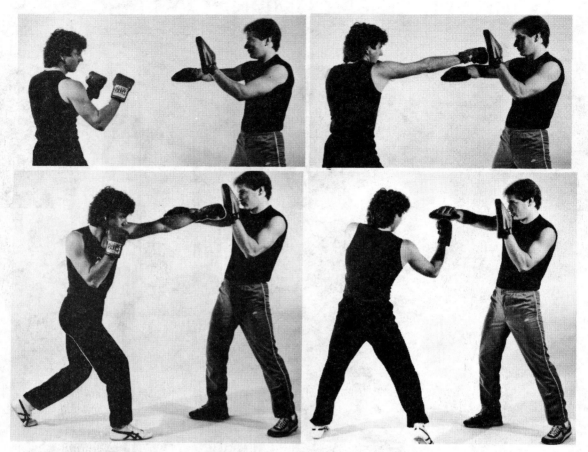

Some of the other stationary combinations you can practice are as follows:

1. Low Jab, High Lead Hook.
2. High Jab, Low Jab, High Hook.
3. High Jab, High Hook, Rear Uppercut.
4. High Jab, Rear Uppercut, High Hook.
5. High Jab, High Lead Hook, Rear Hook.
6. High Jab, Low Lead Hook, High Lead Hook.
7. Low Jab, Rear Hook.
8. Lead Uppercut, Rear High Hook.
9. Lead Hook, Lead Uppercut, Rear Hook.
10. Lead Uppercut, Rear Hook, Lead Hook.
11. Double Jab, any other Hit or Hits.
12. Lead Hook, Rear Hook, Lead Uppercut, Rear Uppercut.
13. Lead Uppercut, Lead Hook, Rear Uppercut, Rear Hook.
14. Cross to Body, High Lead Hook, Cross.
15. Cross to Body, Lead Hook to Body, Cross.

H-F AND F-H USING FOCUS GLOVES

Below are a few of the many combinations.

Jab to Hook Kick

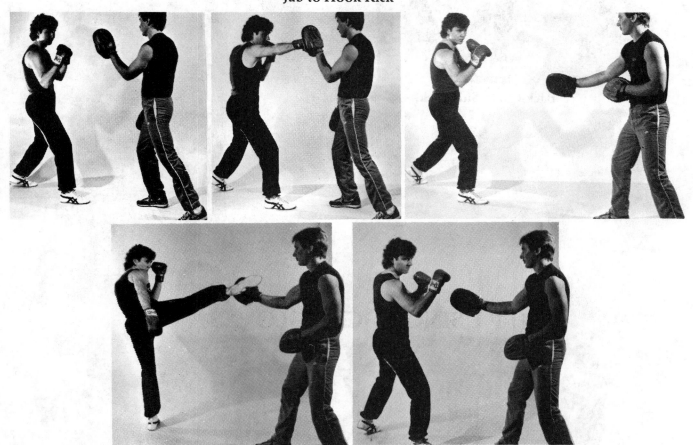

Hook Kick to Jab

Back-Fist to Side Kick

H-H-F USING FOCUS GLOVES

Jab to Cross to Rear Hook Kick

PROGRESSIVE INDIRECT ATTACK (PIA)

Progressive indirect attack is differentiated from attack by combination in that, in PIA, only the final blow is intended to score. This method of attack can be very effective against an opponent whose defense is strong and fast, and who cannot be reached with simple attacks.

PIA uses feints and false attacks to draw a reaction from the opponent, to induce the execution of a block or some other defensive motion, then deceive the defensive move to score in an opening line.

PROGRESSIVE COVER DISTANCE:

Which means that your initial feint or false attack should bridge the distance to be closed by at least half, leaving your final motion only the last half of the distance.

INDIRECT COVERS TIME

You keep ahead of the opponent's defensive move, avoiding contact with the opponent on the feint as you complete your attack. But your feint must be made deep enough, and held long enough, so that the opponent will react to it.

It should be remembered that a progressive indirect attack is a single forward motion without withdrawal. Feints can be simple or compound, but too many motions allow too much time for the opponent to recover or counterattack. Subtlety is an essential ingredient for success—your final motion being economical and fast.

The opponent should be studied first with single attacks and feints to gain some idea as to how he will react in certain situations. The idea is to draw the opponent's defense in the opposite direction from where you want your final attack to land.

A danger of using PIA too frequently is that an opponent may appear to react a certain way during your feints, but then switch and counterattack on your real attack.

Progressive Indirect Attack (PIA) compared to Indirect Attack (IA).

INDIRECT ATTACK (IA)

An indirect attack will usually occur in two motions, the fake and the hit. In the example below a low punch is started toward the target (the fake). Then the fist is withdrawn and a high punch (the hit) is thrown.

PROGRESSIVE INDIRECT ATTACK (PIA)

With a PIA attack, the low punch does not withdraw, rather "progresses" toward the target. With a PIA the two motions are a part of the same motion.

The most common PIA attacks have the following variations:

1. From the low line to the high line
2. From the high line to the low line
3. From the inside line to the outside line
4. From the outside line to the inside line

Below are a few examples of some PIA attacks.

HAND-HAND (H-H) PIA ATTACKS

Low Jab to High Jab

Low Jab to High Hook

Low Jab to Back Fist

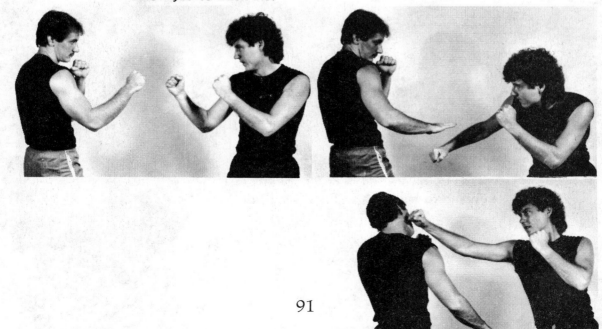

HAND-FOOT (H-F) PIA ATTACKS
Finger Jab to Hook Kick

The hand does not withdraw before the kick.

Finger Jab to Shin Kick

The hand does not withdraw before the kick.

HAND-HAND-FOOT (H-H-F) PIA ATTACKS

Low Jab to High Jab to Rear Leg Hook Kick

Low Jab to High Jab to Side Kick

FOOTWORK TO PIA ATTACKS

Stationary to Stationary with Hit

Step to Stationary with Hit

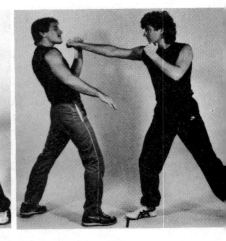

Stationary to Step with Hit

Step to Step with Hit

Which footwork you use depends on distance between you and your opponent.

DEFENSIVE TOOLS AND DRILLS

There is a basic theory in fighting which states, "For every move there is a counter." Attack has been given priority in JKD, and is important, but so is defense. Defensive techniques can negate an opponent's attack and place you in a position to counter. The learning of defensive skills is necessary, and should include as wide a variety of defensive techniques as possible.

One of the main theories of defense in JKD is that the best form of defense is a good offense. Rather than attempting to block a kick or punch, the idea is to try to intercept it with your own kick or punch. This way even if the opponent's attack should score, at least there is an exchange. This requires a continual alertness and awareness of the opponent and his movements.

However, intercepting may not always be possible or appropriate. Perhaps one's awareness is off, you may not have time, then one's skill in defense may well make the difference between success and failure.

The basic methods of defense are listed, from the least to most efficient:

(1) Distance—Simply getting out of the way of the attack and allowing it to miss its target. This usually means that you will not be able to counterattack without first reclosing the distance.

(2) Blocking and Hitting—What is known as "touch and go." In this case the attack is halted with a definite blocking motion, and then the counterattack is launched.

(3) Parrying and Hitting—Differentiated from the previous method by the fact that rather than a pure block, a parry is used to dissolve or redirect the attack, then the counterattack is thrown.

(4) Evasiveness—Includes such body motions as slipping, ducking, bobbing and weaving in order to avoid an attack by misplacement, while remaining in range to counter.

(5) Intercepting—The opponent's attack is intercepted by the defender's own counterattack, nullifying the original attack.

As stated before, the method of defense chosen may depend upon the circumstances under which an attack is delivered. Sometimes distance may be more appropriate than interception, and vice versa. If you understand all the variables, you have a wider selection to choose from and will not be limited.

The following sequences offer examples of the defensive methods just described, with the exception of distance.

BLOCKING AND HITTING
SHOULDER STOP AGAINST WIDE REAR CROSS

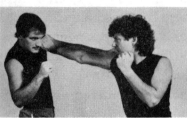

As the opponent starts to throw a wide rear cross, the defender snaps out his lead hand to shove the opponent's shoulder, disrupting the opponent's punch, then counters immediately with his own rear cross.

Closeup insert of shoulder stop (can be used on opponent's bicep if shoulder is too far away).

SHOULDER STOP AGAINST REAR OVERHEAD

As opponent launches a rear overhead, the defender uses the same shoulder stop. (Note defender's rear hand is kept well up and guarding against opponent's possible lead hand punch.)

CUT INTO REAR UPPERCUT

As opponent throws a rear uppercut to the solar plexus, the defender lowers his lead elbow and wedges his lead arm onto the uppercut, then immediately counters with a rear uppercut. (Note how defender keeps himself covered and is aware of opponent's other hand.)

FOREARM BLOCK FRONT UPPERCUT

As opponent loops a lead uppercut to the solar plexus, the defender twists his body, dropping his rear forearm into the crook of the opponent's elbow, smothering the punch, immediately follows with a lead hook to the opponent's head.

COVER AGAINST LEAD HOOK
TO HEAD

As opponent throws a high lead hook, defender shifts forward into the circumference of the blow, and covers with his rear hand, immediately follows with his own lead hook counter. (Be very aware of opponent's rear hand and elbow when you are in this position.)

PARRYING AND HITTING
OUTSIDE PARRY AND HIT BODY

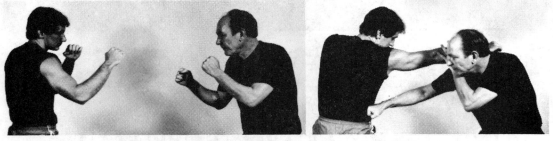

Opponent throws a lead jab. Just before it lands defender uses a cross parry with his rear hand, deflecting the punch over his lead shoulder while returning a low lead punch to opponent's stomach (defender shifts his body slightly left as an added safety measure).

OUTSIDE PARRY AND HIT HEAD
(INSIDE)

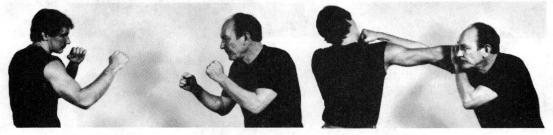

Same parry as above but this time the defender returns a high lead punch inside opponent's guard.

OUTSIDE PARRY AND HIT HEAD (OUTSIDE)

Sometimes an opponent will drop his lead after punching. This time as the opponent throws his lead jab, defender uses a rear cross parry, but returns his own high lead to the outside of opponent's lead arm.

INSIDE PARRY AND HIT HEAD

The lead jab is deflected with the rear hand as the defender shifts to the inside position and counters with his own lead jab. (Be careful anytime you move to the inside position as you are vulnerable to opponent's rear hand.)

CROSS PARRY AND FINGER JAB

As the lead jab is thrown, defender twists his upper body as he uses a lead hand cross parry and counters with a rear hand finger jab to opponent's eyes.

DOUBLE LOW PARRY

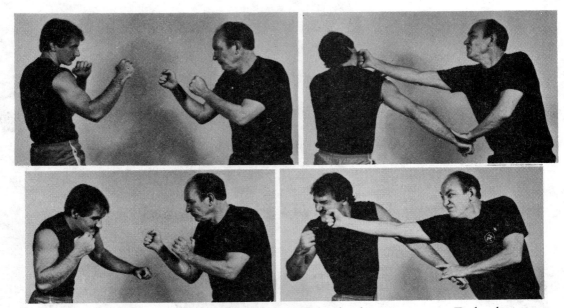

Opponent attempts to throw a low lead jab—rear cross. Defender parrys the jab with his rear hand and counter jabs with his lead hand. As rear cross is thrown he uses the same rear hand parry while countering with another lead punch.

PASS AND UPPERCUT

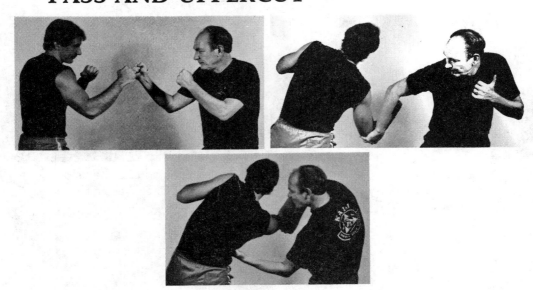

As opponent throws a shovel hook, defender drops lead hand, cupping opponent's arm and sweeping it outwards, then counters with his own shovel hook. (Sometimes combined with a sidestep to increase safety factor.)

EVASION
SLIP OUTSIDE

Opponent throws a lead jab. Just before impact the defender slips to the outside position, displacing his body from the punch, and is ready to counter.

SLIP INSIDE

Defender slips to the inside position, ready to counter. (Note high guard position in case opponent throws rear hand.)

SLIP OUTSIDE WITH COVER

the defender uses a rear hand cover as an added safety factor.

SLIP INSIDE WITH COVER

the defender uses a lead hand cover as an added safety factor.

DUCKING

FRONT HOOK

Defender ducks under opponent's lead hook by bending legs and shifting trunk slightly forward, hands held high and eyes watching opponent, ready to counter with either hand or defend.

REAR HOOK

Defender ducks under rear hook using the same motion as previously described, allows the blow to continue on its way, ready to counter or defend as necessary.

(In ducking one should be aware of not only possible hand follow-ups by the opponent, but also use of the rear leg, knee or elbow.)

(USING DISTANCE)
SNAP AWAY AGAINST JAB

As opponent flicks out a lead jab, defender shifts weight to his rear leg as he snaps his upper body out of distance and prepares to cover with his rear hand if necessary.

Note: This must be an extremely fast motion, otherwise there is a danger of being caught by a rear cross.

SHOULDER ROLL AGAINST REAR CROSS

As opponent's rear cross comes out, the defender shifts his weight to his rear leg and rolls backwards away from the punch. The chin is kept well tucked, behind the lead shoulder, eyes watching the opponent, arms covering the body and face.

103

BOBBING AND WEAVING

The following sequence of photographs illustrate the basic body mechanics of the bob and weave against an opponent, in matched leads.

To the outside

From the ready position, and making it one smooth motion, bob forward by bending at the knees and waist, hands high and well covered, ready to slip at any time if necessary. Then weave to the outside position, ready to counter. Sometimes a sidestep is added with the weave to achieve a more favorable position to counter.

To the inside

The mechanics are the same as above only this time you weave to the inside position.

BOB AND WEAVE TO OUTSIDE AGAINST LEAD HOOK

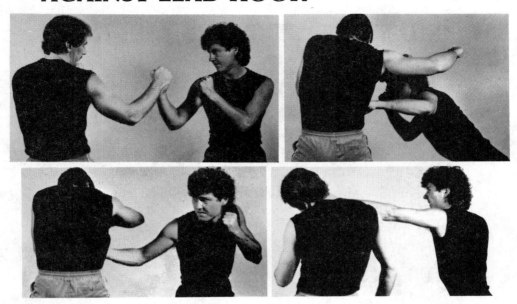

As opponent launches a lead hook bob forward to the inside position, hitting midsection with a tight rear cross (or hook), weave to the outside position and score with a body hook, followed immediately by a high rear cross.

BOB AND WEAVE AGAINST REAR CROSS

Opponent throws a high rear cross, defender bobs to the inside position and scores with a lead straight punch to the opponent's midsection, then weaves to the outside position and scores with a rear uppercut.

INTERCEPTION

An intercepting hit and parry can be done three ways.

COVER AND THEN HIT

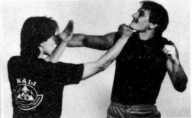

Opponent throws a lead jab. Defender covers the line and returns his own lead punch.

SIMULTANEOUS COVER AND HIT

This time defender covers the lead jab of the opponent and returns his own lead punch simultaneously.

HIT FOLLOWED BY COVER

This time the defender anticipates the opponent's lead jab and beats him to the punch, then covers the opponent's jab as a follow-up if necessary.

STOP KICK AGAINST LEAD JAB

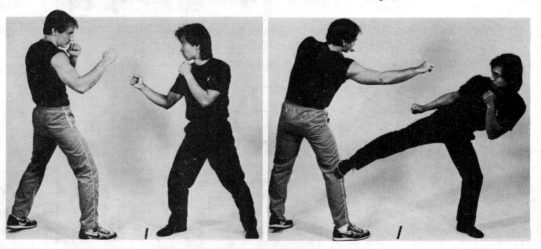

As opponent throws a lead jab, defender intercepts his attack with a stop-kick to the knee while shifting his own body out of range of the jab.

STOP HIT AGAINST KICK

As opponent launches a rear hook kick, defender intercepts his attack with a lead straight punch to the face.

STOP HIT AGAINST KICK WITH LOW COVER

Same as above only this time the defender closes the distance and covers the low line as he hits.

STOP KICK AGAINST KICK

As opponent launches a rear straight kick, defender counters by intercepting his attack with a stop kick to the opponent's leg.

SLIDING LEVERAGE AGAINST JAB

As opponent jabs, defender bridges across the outside of opponent's arm, simultaneously deflecting the punch and countering with a finger jab to the eyes. (This is a sliding motion which maintains contact with opponent's arm throughout.)

SLIDING LEVERAGE AGAINST REAR CROSS

As opponent throws a rear cross, defender bridges across the opponent's arm with his own rear sliding leverage, simultaneously deflecting the blow and countering.

SLIDING LEVERAGE AGAINST UPPERCUT

As opponent launches a lead uppercut to the midsection, defender lowers his body slightly, cuts into the punch and counters with his own punch.

CATCH AND RETURN JAB

As opponent jabs, defender catches the punch with his rear guard hand, then returns his own jab as the opponent's arm retracts.

SIMULTANEOUS CATCH AND JAB

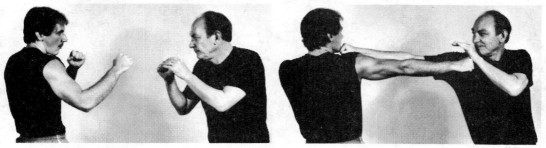

This time the catch and return jabs are used simultaneously.

CATCH AND CROSS PARRY AGAINST JAB AND CROSS

As opponent jabs to the low line, defender simultaneously catches and returns a high jab, then cross parrys the opponent's low cross while scoring with another high straight punch.

COUNTER ATTACKING

A counterattack is an attack made as the opponent is attacking, or is about to. It can be divided into three timings.

(1) **Before the movement**—While the opponent is preparing to launch an attack (attack on preparation) possibly by advancing with footwork.

(2) **During the movement**—While the attack is under development but has not reached its target (outgoing).

(3) **After the movement**—As the attack reaches complete extension, or even as it is retracting (chambering).

The following sequence of photographs illustrates the various timings as used against a lead jab-rear cross attack.

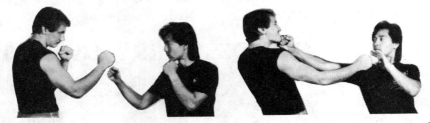

As opponent begins to throw the lead jab, defender counterattacks before and intercepts motion with his own lead punch, thus nullifying the attack at the start.

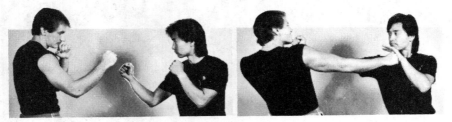

This time the defender simultaneously catches the jab and counters with his own jab.

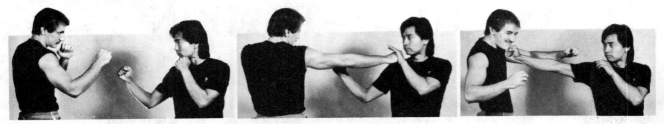

The defender catches the opponent's lead jab, then stop-hits as the cross is coming.

The lead jab is caught and the defender simultaneously parries the rear cross and hits.

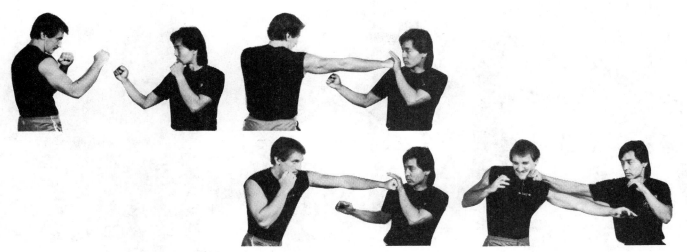

The defender catches the lead jab and rear cross, then counters to the opponent's face.

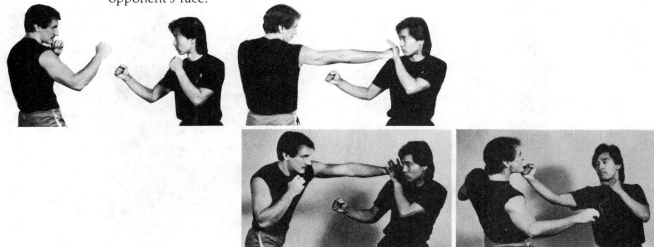

The defender catches the jab, parries the rear cross, then counter hits.

USING FOOT DEFENSIVE TOOLS

As opponent is beginning to initiate a kicking attack, the defender intercepts the attack with a stop-kick, followed by a finger jab as the distance is closed.

As the opponent's kick is on its way, the defender uses footwork and body angulation to avoid the kicking leg and cuts the opponent's support leg with a counter kick.

As opponent side kicks, defender closes range and parries the kick while simultaneously stop-kicking opponent's support leg.

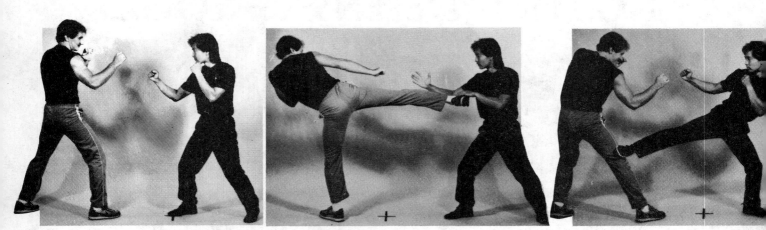

If opponent pendulum side kicks, defender pendulum shifts back and parries the kick as it reaches full extension, then follows with a pendulum side kick to opponent's returning leg.

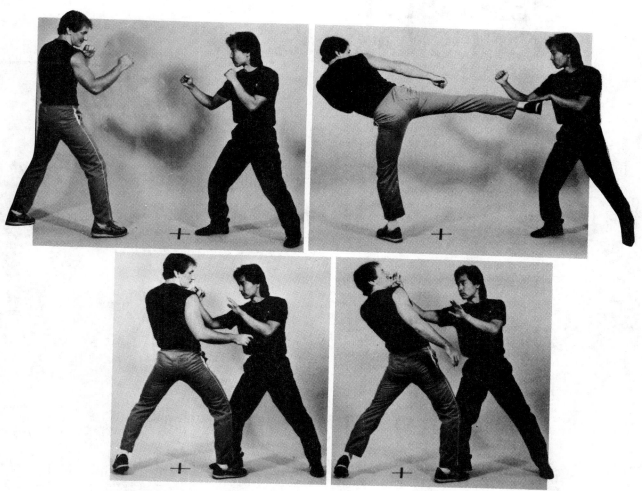

If opponent side kicks and plants his weight forward, defender uses a slide-step retreat and parries the kick at full extension, then crashes opponent's line with a lead punch.

Timing and distance are important if you want to be in range to counterattack successfully.

The same defensive concepts illustrated can be used against combination attacks using: hand-foot, foot-foot, or foot-hand attacks.

DEFENSIVE USE OF FOCUS GLOVE

The focus glove can also be used to:

1. **Block and counterattack.**
2. **To check your cover.**
3. **To work on slipping and the bob and weave.**

Some examples of the defensive use of focus gloves:

Inside parry the jab to jab

When your training partner jabs or does a loose hook with the front focus glove, bring up your rear hand to inside parry the attack then return a jab.

Shoulder roll the cross to return cross and uppercut.

When your partner hits you with a rear focus glove, put your weight on your rear leg and roll away from the punch. Quickly return a cross followed by an uppercut.

Jab to cover low cross.

After you jab your partner returns a low cross. Quickly bring your elbow down to cover the punch.

Jab to cover low jab.

After you jab, your partner returns a low jab. Cover it with your rear elbow.

Inside slip the jab to high hook

When your partner jabs, slip inside the jab and return a high hook. Notice how the man who jabs returns the glove to hook position.

Outside slip jab to cross

Slip outside of the jab and return a cross.

Bob and weave under front hook to low hook and cross return.

When your partner does a hook with the focus glove, bob to the inside. Then quickly weave under the arm, hook to the body as you come up from the weave. Follow this with a cross.

Bob and weave under rear hook to uppercut, hook

Bob inside his rear hook. Weave to the outside, then uppercut the body and hook to the focus glove.

116

Cover low hook to double uppercut.

When your partner does a low hook, cover it with your rear elbow followed by two uppercuts.

You should practice all of the above until you can react instantly. Then you should mix the drills so that you block and hit or hit and then block. Be as inventive as possible. Work the focus gloves until you and your partner make it as close to sparring as possible.

ATTACK BY DRAWING (ABD)

Attack by drawing is essentially counterfighting. It is initiated by "baiting" an opponent into a commitment. By offering him an apparent opening, or by executing an action that he may attempt to time and counter, and then to counterattack as he "takes the bait."

You can draw an opponent's commitment by:

(a) Exposing a target to the opponent (invitation).

(b) Forcing a reaction (as in crashing a particular line).

(c) Feinting (to draw a reaction).

The first method (invitation) is DEFENSIVE—in that the intent is to cause the opponent to attack under certain conditions so as to know the exact sector the attack will arrive in. The other methods (forcing and feinting) are OFFENSIVE—in that the intention is to make the opponent react in a set manner and to develop an attack that takes into account either his defensive move or his counterattack.

In fencing, ABD is referred to as second-intention attack, and is very effective against a fighter who bases his game plan primarily on counterattack.

An important point to remember is that attack by drawing is a premeditated action and its success depends upon luring the opponent into attacking into the opening being offered. Subtlety is an essential ingredient then, for the action must achieve the desired result, that of drawing a specific reaction from the opponent. And though it must be a deliberate error, it must never appear so to the opponent or he will not take the opening. (Very experienced fighters will seldom, if ever, attack into an open sector if they have the slightest idea that it may be a setup.)

Correct timing and distance are extremely important in using ABD. If you are too close to the opponent, his attack may score before you have time to counter, and if you are too far away he may not react to the opening, or even if he does, distance will not allow your own counterattack to score.

Balance is necessary in your attack also, so as to be ready to counterattack or defend yourself if necessary.

The following examples illustrate various ways of using attack by drawing.

DIFFERENT HAND "BAITS."

The photos below show the "baits" in exaggerated form for clarity.

Defender lowers rear hand guard to expose head.   Defender lowers lead hand guard to expose head.   Defender raises rear elbow to expose body.

Defender raises both elbows to expose body.   Defender holds both hands wide to expose interior body and head.

ATTACK BY DRAWING
AGAINST HANDS

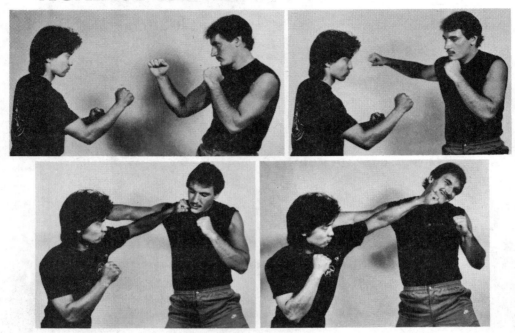

Defender lowers his rear hand guard slightly, drawing a lead hook from his opponent, which he counters by sidestepping and throwing a rear cross to opponent's face (lead hand held high to counter opponent's rear hand).

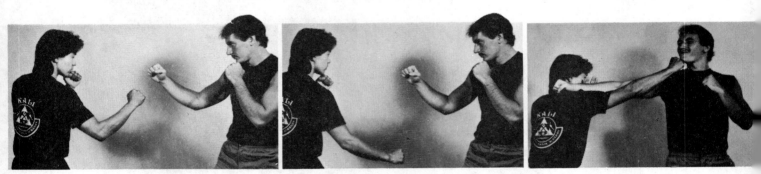

Defender lowers his lead hand to draw a lead punch from the opponent, which he counters by slipping outside and returning a high jab.

Dropping his lead hand, the defender baits the opponent's lead jab, then slips inside and counters with a rear cross to opponent's midsection.

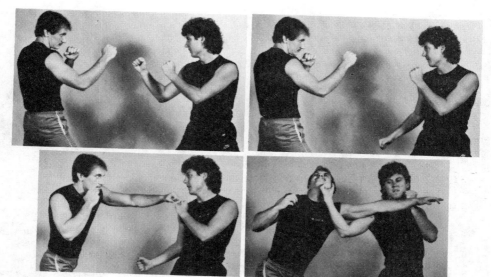

Lowering his lead hand, the defender baits a high rear cross, which he counters by angling his body and scoring with a lead uppercut to opponent's jaw (or body).

Defender lowers his rear guard while throwing a lead jab, baiting his opponent's lead hook counter, which the defender sidesteps while throwing a rear uppercut to opponent's jaw (or body).

Defender lowers his rear guard while throwing a lead jab, drawing opponent's lead hook counter, which the defender simultaneously parries while scoring with a lead punch.

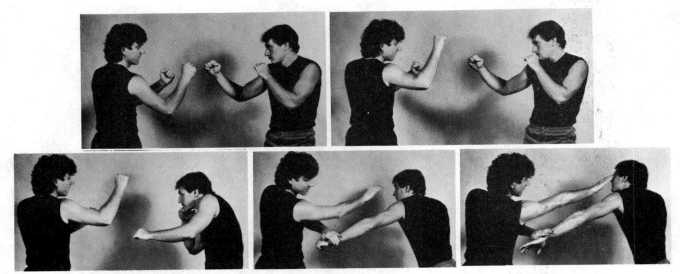

Defender raises lead arm to draw opponent's low rear cross, which he counters with a rear hand parry while simultaneously shooting a finger jab to opponent's eyes.

ATTACK BY DRAWING AGAINST FEET

Defender exposes ribcage to draw opponent's lead hook kick, which he counters by simultaneously parrying the kick while scoring with a rear cross to opponent's face. (Note that defender moves inside the circumference of the kick.)

Defender lowers rear guard to bait opponent's high lead hook kick, which he counters by sidestepping and cutting into opponent's support leg with his own rear hook kick. (Upper body is angulated to avoid kicking leg of opponent.)

Defender exposes body to draw opponent's rear hook kick, which he counters by crashing inside with a lead punch to opponent's face.

One danger in using attack by drawing is that if the opponent suspects he is being baited, he may appear to react to the motion, then counter your attack himself. Therefore it should be used sparingly and judiciously, and should be accompanied by body angulation and a well-covered position in attack.

Used in conjunction with all other ways of attack and with defensive motions, ABD adds variety to your fighting tactics.

KICKBOXING TRAINING DRILLS

Sparring is a matter of choices. Choosing the right weapon to use, finding the correct distance in relation to the opponent, choosing the right moment to attack or defend. Sparring, broken down to its essence, is about timing and distance.

You may have all of the physical tools at your disposal, but if you are not in range to use them, they won't do you any good. Likewise, if you have the tools and the proper distance, but your timing is incorrect, your attack will be less than sure of success.

In learning to kickbox, the initial stage the martial artist concentrates his efforts upon is the development of physical skills. Through constant drilling of precise actions, the fighter conditions his reflexes and reactions to respond immediately to the situation at hand. This conditioning is known as transferring an action from volitional to reflex action—from having to think about it to its becoming reflex. The fighter's choice of action is dependent upon the variety of responses he has conditioned into his neuromuscular system. If he has learned a wide range of reflexive actions, he has a greater choice.

Each physical skill must be learned first, the same way one learns any lesson. But it must be taken beyond that initial level. Automaticity of response is what is desired, where the skill has become second nature to the individual. Then the fighter can concentrate on tactics.

However, "non-thinking" repetition can produce a "robotic" mechanical reaction, rather than relating to the opponent. In training, therefore, quality is to be more valued than simple, non-thinking quantity.

In training with drills, an important point to remember is that both people are learning while drilling. Each training partner must carry out the actions genuinely, remembering that they are assisting each other in developing proper body mechanics, learning proper timing and distance, while increasing the speed at which the drill is being practiced.

To be functional, any sparring should approach reality and approximate combat as closely as possible, which means it must eventually be done at full combat speed. (Techniques with full coordination and increasing speed—precision in all.)

The sparring drills offered in this chapter are only a few of many, and are designed to help a martial artist increase self-confidence while developing a physical skill. Total, unrestricted sparrring is the ultimate choice in Jeet Kune Do.

CATCH DRILLS

The purpose of using a catch against the first punch is to enable you to "gauge the distance" between yourself and the opponent. In all of the following drills you can hit on the first motion if you are able to.

CATCH LEAD JAB—RETURN DRILLS

One man initiates with a high lead jab, partner catches the jab and returns a high lead jab.

One man initiates with a high lead jab, partner catches the jab and returns a low lead jab.

One man initiates with a high lead jab, partner catches the jab and returns a high backfist.

One man initiates with a high lead jab, partner catches the jab and returns a high loose hook.

Closeup of cover

CATCH JAB—
COUNTER REAR CROSS DRILLS

One man initiates a high jab—rear cross combination. Partner catches the jab, catches the cross. (May require backward movement at the same time.)

Defender catches the jab, shoulder rolls away from the rear cross.

Defender catches the jab, uses a shoulder stop against the rear cross. (Usually used against a wide, looping rear cross.)

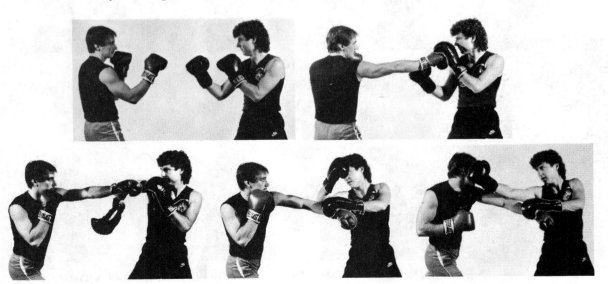

Defender catches the jab, uses a Boang Sao deflection against the rear cross, then traps the opponent's arm and backfists.

Defender catches the jab, slips outside the rear cross and counters to opponent's midsection.

Defender catches the jab, slips inside the rear cross and counters with a low lead jab. (Be aware of opponent's lead hand when on the inside position.)

Defender catches the jab, counters with a lead hook over the opponent's rear cross while shifting backwards. (Good if opponent leans forward with rear cross.)

Defender catches the jab, slips to the outside while countering the cross with a lead uppercut to opponent's jaw. (Usually used against a straight rear cross.)

Defender catches the jab, leans back and side kicks into opponent's knee as rear cross is thrown. (Keep rear hand guard well covered as you kick.)

Defender catches the jab, leans back and hook kicks into opponent's ribs as rear cross is thrown. (Keep rear hand guard high.)

CATCH JAB— COUNTER LEAD HOOK DRILLS

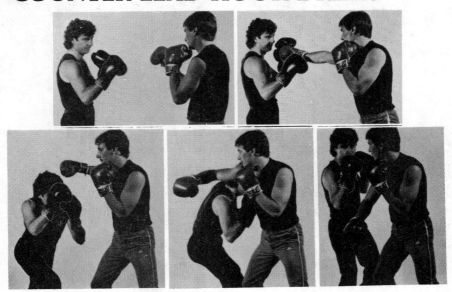

Defender catches the jab, bobs and weaves under the lead hook to the outside of opponent's lead.

Defender catches the jab, shifts inside the circumference of the lead hook while covering with the rear guard hand.

Defender catches the jab, extends rear hand to palm stop into opponent's lead hooking bicep (note high lead hand guard to defend against possible rear hand punch from opponent).

Closeup of palm stop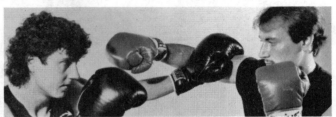

Defender catches the jab, then sidesteps, angling his body while intercepting opponent's lead hook with a rear cross to opponent's jaw (or body).

CATCH JAB—
COUNTER FRONT UPPERCUT DRILLS

Defender catches the jab, lowers rear forearm to wedge into the crook of opponent's elbow as he attempts a front uppercut.

Defender catches the jab, scoops opponent's lead uppercut aside with his lead hand, counters with a shovel hook to opponent's ribs.

Defender catches the jab, shoots his own rear uppercut on top of opponent's lead uppercut, smothering the punch.

Defender catches the jab, angles his body and shoots a rear uppercut under the opponent's uppercut to deflect the blow.

CATCH DRILL VARIATIONS

Defender catches the jab and simultaneously returns his own lead jab.

Defender catches the jab, returns a rear cross counter to opponent's jaw.

4 CORNER TRAINING

The following photographs illustrate the basic 4 Corner parries using the rear hand guard.

Front view

Side view

High Outside Gate

Defender parries opponent's rear cross using a high cross parry (Woang Pak), while simultaneously scoring with a lead punch to opponent's face.

High Inside Gate

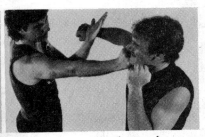

Defender parries opponent's long lead hook using a high inside parry (Tan Sao) while simultaneously countering with a straight lead to opponent's face. (Do not attempt to use this against a tight boxing hook.)

Low Outside Gate

Defender parries opponent's low rear cross using a low outside slapping parry (Ouy Ha Pak) while simultaneously countering with a lead punch to opponent's face.

Low Inside Gate

Defender parries a long low hook using a semicircular parry (Loy Ha Pak) and counters simultaneously with a lead punch to opponent's face.

The same 4 corner parries can be done using the lead guard hand.

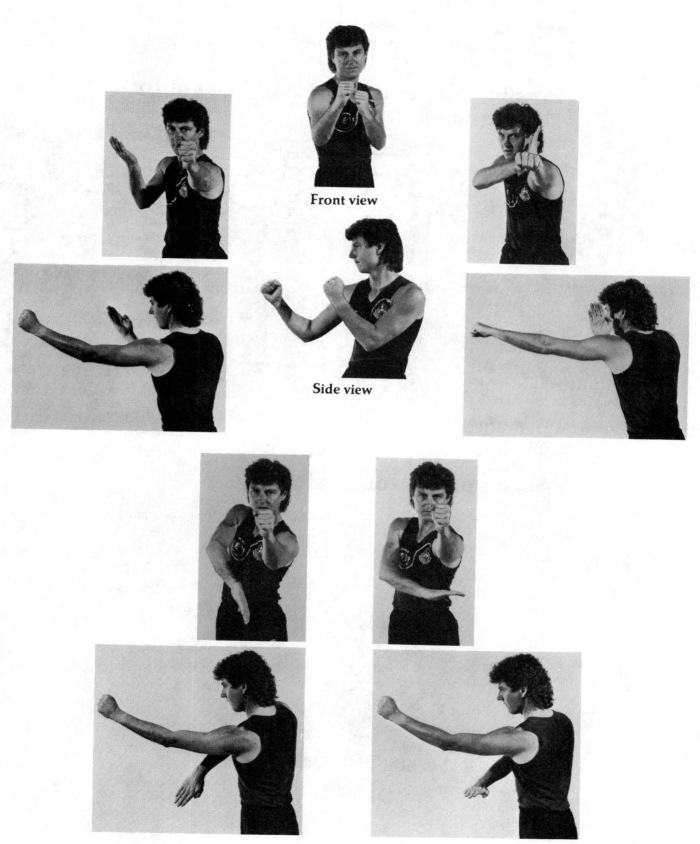

Front view

Side view

4 corner parries can be done three ways:

1. **Parry followed by hit.**
2. **Parry and hit simultaneously.**
3. **Hit followed by parry.**

Possible Angles of Rear Hand Guard for High Inside Parry

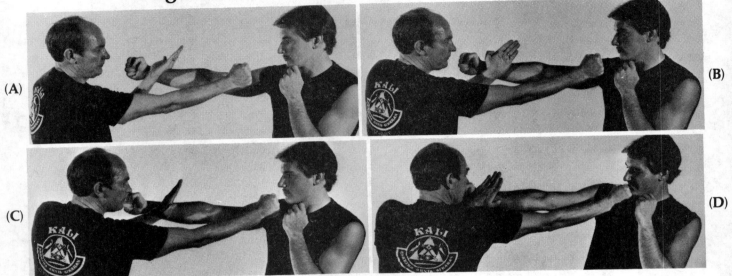

(A)

(B)

(C)

(D)

The above photographs illustrate the possible positions that the rear hand may be angled at while using a high inside parry. (**A**) Palm supinated. (**B**) Palm half-supinated. (**C**) Palm pronated. (**D**) Palm half-pronated.

Angles of Fist for Parries

The use of a particular parry is dependent upon which sector a blow is traveling in.

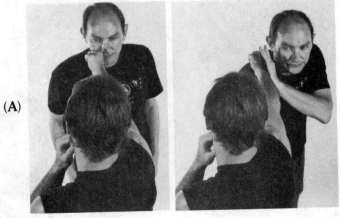

(A)

Above photographs illustrate which sector the opponent's punch should be in in order to effectively use a high rear cross parry.

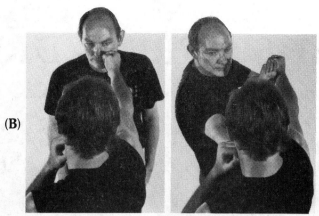

(B)

When the punch is traveling in this sector, one can use a high rear inside parry.

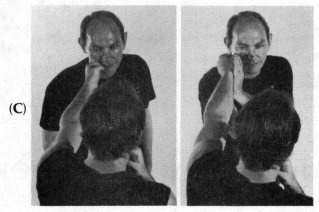

(C)

This time an opponent's rear hand punch is traveling into the same sector as shown in (**A**), and is parried with the same high rear cross parry.

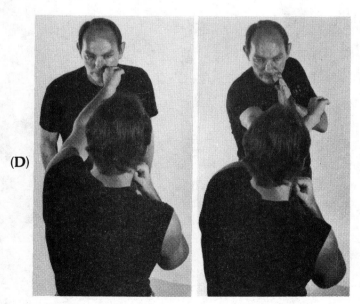

(D)

When the opponent's rear punch is traveling in the same sector as shown in (**B**), the defender bridges across the punching arm. This is referred to as "cutting into the opponent's tool."

FOOT SPARRING DRILLS
DOUBLE PURSUING HOOK KICK

Partner initiates a step and slide lead hook kick. As opponent shifts out of range while maintaining the same lead, partner closes the distance immediately with a second lead hook kick to score.

LEAD HOOK KICK TO REAR HOOK KICK

This time as partner attempts to close the distance with a step and slide lead hook kick, opponent shifts back out of range and switches leads. Partner plants kicking leg forward and shoots an immediate rear hook kick to opponent.

ANGLING AGAINST LEAD HOOK KICK

As opponent initiates a sliding lead hook kick, partner angles his body away from the kick with a sidestep, and cuts opponent's support leg with a rear hook kick.

ANGLING AGAINST REAR HOOK KICK

As opponent launches a high rear hook kick, partner angles away from the kick using a sidestep, and cuts opponent's support leg with a lead hook kick.

USING A PENDULUM RETREAT
AGAINST SIDE KICK—RETURN

As opponent slides in with a side kick, defender pendulum retreats and parries the kick as it reaches full extension, returns a slide lead side kick and closes range.

Same as before only this time the defender returns a slide lead hook kick.

EXCHANGE KICK FOR KICK DRILLS

The purpose of these drills is to parry the opponent's kick and return your own kick as quickly as possible, which he then parries. Usually the drills are practiced in a sequence of either two or three kicks in order to create a rapid-fire exchange.

HOOK KICK EXCHANGE

Opponent initiates with a lead hook kick, which defender parries and immediately returns his own lead hook kick which opponent must parry.

SIDE KICK EXCHANGE

Same as above only this time a side kick is used.

REAR HOOK KICK EXCHANGE

Opponent initiates with a rear hook kick, which the defender parries with a knee raise, and immediately returns his own rear hook kick which opponent must then parry.

COMBINING HANDS AND FEET

As the martial artist progresses and begins to feel comfortable in using his punching and kicking tools, he should begin to combine hands and feet in sparring and drilling, learning how to put combinations together, and developing the ability to shift unconsciously from one to the other as necessary.

TYPES OF OPPONENTS

There are various types of opponents one must learn to deal with. The following sequence of photographs illustrates the different types of opponent one may encounter, and the various distances each type may use.

A Runner

This type of opponent is "flighty" and anytime you try to initiate an attack runs away out of distance of both hands and feet.

One Who Guards With Distance

This opponent uses distance to stay outside of any hand or foot attack, but remains closer than the runner, awaiting an opportunity to score or counter.

One Who Guards and Prepares to Crash (Blocker)

This opponent usually remains well covered and is prepared to block an attack and then counter.

The Jammer

This opponent likes to crash into an attack in order to smother or jam it, and counter. He usually maintains a well-guarded position as he jams.

The Angler

An opponent who likes to use footwork and evasive body angulation to offset an attack.

One can and should learn to deal with every kind of opponent. In this way you will not be surprised by an unfamiliar action.

IN CONCLUSION

The total development of a martial artist is a complex process, for it encompasses so many different aspects. There are physical, mental and emotional differences that all need to be taken into account.

Many people are scared away from certain sports, especially contact sports such as boxing or kickboxing, and generally it is because they have been made to take too many risks too soon. As a result, they feel inadequate, lost, their fears mounting as they feel they are not in control—and eventually they quit.

The solution to this is a process known in sports as "enhancing the safety zone." When a trainer uses this process gradually and professionally, the situation doesn't seem threatening. When dealing with personal risk the martial artist should always be in control of the elements of the activity, for only then can they overcome any fears they may have.

144